Pacer the Pony

Jane Burton

Random House 🏠 New York

With thanks to Dee Bennett, Peggy Lucas, and Carolyn Woods for their help

Text and photographs copyright © 1989 by Jane Burton. Copyright © 1989 by Belitha Press. All rights reserved under International and Pan-American Copyright Conventions. Published in the United States by Random House, Inc., New York.

Library of Congress Cataloging-in-Publication Data:
Burton, Jane. Pacer the pony. (How your pet grows!) SUMMARY: Depicts a pony growing, learning, and playing during the first year of its life on a farm. ISBN: 0-394-82271-4 (pbk.); 0-394-92271-9 (lib. bdg.) 1. Ponies—Juvenile literature. [1. Ponies. 2. Animals—Infancy] I. Title. II. Series: Burton, Jane. How your pet grows! SF315.B86 1989 636.1′617 89-42693

Manufactured in Hong Kong   1 2 3 4 5 6 7 8 9 0

Katie is lying in her stall. But she is not going to sleep. She is very restless. She gets up and lies down again. She is about to have her baby, called a foal.

As soon as her foal is born, Katie nuzzles him, getting to know his smell. She rests awhile, then stands up. Pacer is too new to stand. His mother licks his wet coat to help him dry off.

One hour old

Pacer's long thin legs stick out awkwardly all around him. He struggles and struggles to get up. Every time he is nearly standing, Katie nuzzles him and he topples over again.

At last Pacer is up and balancing on his feet. But when he tries to walk, he just stumbles and staggers. Then he collapses in a heap of jumbled legs again.

One day old

Pacer's coat is dry. Now, when he walks, his feet *usually* take him the way he wants to go. He stays very close to Katie. She keeps nuzzling and smelling him. Every hour he drinks her warm milk.

Ten days old

Today is the first warm day, so the mare and her foal go outdoors. Pacer has never been outside his stable before. Now, suddenly, he has a lot of space around him. His legs are strong and he can run. He runs in dizzy circles around and around his mother. He gallops like a little racehorse until he is puffing so much he has to stop and catch his breath.

Two weeks old

When the weather is nice, the ponies go out into the field. Katie goes straight to the spring grass to eat. Pacer is too young to eat grass. He is still amazed at all the new sights and sounds and smells. He stands and stares and listens and sniffs.

Pacer, curious, follows Clara the cow as she grazes. Head up, tail up! He watches Clara, ready to dash back to Katie if the cow should swing around at him with her horns. But Clara, like Katie, is busy eating grass—too busy to bother with Pacer!

Three weeks old

Pacer's teeth are coming through. He is starting to eat grass. When he has an itch, he gnaws himself gently with his teeth. Sometimes he rolls in the grass to scratch his back. He kicks his legs in the air as he goes over.

There are other pony mares and foals in the field. Each foal stays near its own mother. They watch each other, but their mothers will not let them play together yet.

The only playmate Pacer has is his own mother. He prances around her, biting her neck. But Katie is *not* playful. All she wants to do is eat grass. She puts her ears back to show that she is annoyed.

Pacer is only a baby and needs plenty of rest. When he is tired of prancing and galloping and exploring, he stretches full length in the sun and goes to sleep. Katie grazes close to him, keeping watch. She never leaves him.

One month old

Clara's new calf is napping. Clara is eating grass nearby. Katie goes to smell the new calf, but it gets up in a hurry and runs to its mother. Pacer stays behind Katie so he won't be seen by Clara.

Pacer is napping standing up. Suddenly he wakes up with a start. Something has come up behind him! But it is only Katie, rubbing against him.

A foal has a special way of saying "I am only little. Please don't hurt me." He opens and shuts his mouth, making sucking noises. Big horses understand this signal and do not hurt the foal.

Pacer's father, Fizz, has come to visit. Pacer is afraid of him and stays on the other side of Katie. Fizz reaches over her back to smell Pacer. Fizz would never hurt a little foal.

Two months old

Now that Pacer is growing up, Katie lets him play with the other foals. Amanda gets up when he nudges her to play. But she is a younger filly. The games the older colts play are too rough for her. Amanda scampers back to her mother.

Rusty is *always* ready for a game. He gives Pacer a playful nip. Pacer tosses his head and starts to run. Together they chase around the field, bucking and kicking playfully. Sometimes they rear up and box each other with their front feet. The two colts have a great game.

Four months old

Pacer has lost his fluffy foal coat. His mane and tail are growing. He needs that long tail to swish away the flies.

Some kinds of flies just walk on the ponies. They tickle! Pacer tosses his head to shake off the little pests.

Other kinds of flies are stingers. Ponies really hate stinging flies. They panic when they hear them coming. Katie and Pacer run and hide where it is too cool and dark for the flies.

Five months old

Summer nights are pleasant for ponies. The pesty flies are asleep. The ponies sleep for part of the night too. Just before dawn they wake up hungry and start grazing again. They munch dark paths through the dewy grass. When they are not dozing, they are eating. Pacer is always hungry—as hungry as a horse!

As the sun rises, Pacer and Katie make their way up to the top of the hill. They stand in the sun to warm up after the cool of the night.

Six months old

A pony is often afraid of walking into water. He needs to see where he is putting his feet. When Pacer was a little foal, he would never step into a puddle. He always walked around it.

There has been so much rain that Pacer's field is flooded. Now he thinks it's fun to slosh through puddles and blow on the water.

Every day Pacer rolls in mud. He shakes himself afterward. Some of the mud flies off him, but most of it sticks to his coat.

Nine months old

Charlie the cat is on his way home from a hunting trip. Pacer follows him across the field, sniffing at his bushy tail. Charlie jumps onto the fence and gets ready to swat Pacer on the nose.

Joy, the gray mare, has a blanket on to keep her warm. Pacer doesn't need a blanket. His own thick woolly winter coat keeps him warm.

Pacer keeps eating grass while the snow is falling. When the sun comes out again, Pacer has a blanket on too—a blanket of snow!

One year old

It is spring again. Pacer is no longer a foal. He is a yearling colt. He has learned to wear a bridle and walk on a lead line.

Every day Pacer is brushed until his chestnut coat gleams. Today his mane and tail have been braided, too. His socks—the white parts of his legs—have been washed so there is no trace of mud on them. He is going to a pony show.

Perhaps one day Pacer will be a champion like his father. He will win prizes at many shows, just because he is such a beautiful pony.